A Vision for Rational High-Growth Management in Upstate South Carolina

Dennis C. Hayes
Chairman of SpartansFirst

SpartansFirst
Press

This volume presents a policy discussion intended for informational and civic education purposes. It is not legal, engineering, financial, zoning, or planning advice.

Published by SpartansFirst Press

Errata: Errors@journeymanpublishing.com

First Edition, 2026.   Paperback: 978-1-964222-08-0
                        e-book: 978-1-964222-09-7

SpartansFirst Press is an imprint of Journeyman Publishing LLC. The SpartansFirst logo is the service mark for the SpartansFirst Not for Profit corporation. It's use on this book is with permission of the board for specific publications.

Journeyman Publishing's logo & the JP Signet are registered trademarks of Journeyman Publishing, LLC. Other product and company names mentioned herein may be trademarks of their respective owners. Rather than use a trademark symbol on everything as it appears, we are using the names in an editorial fashion only to the benefit of the trademark owner. There is no intention to infringe on an existing or retired trademark.

This book is distributed "as is, where is," without any warranty, explicit or implied. While every precaution has been taken in the preparation of this work, neither the author nor Journeyman Publishing LLC shall have any liability to any person or entity with respect to any loss or damages caused or alleged to be caused directly or indirectly by the information contained.

SpartansFirst Press focuses on issues related to items at the intersection of governance, public policy, and technology. Journeyman Publishing is a specialty publisher for Cybersecurity, IT Professional Services, Software Performance Engineering, Technical Selling, & Software Quality Assurance books. If you have an interest in becoming a published writer, please contact us at newauthor@journeymanpublishing.com

Printed in the United States of America

Journeyman Publishing   111 Foster Mill Circle, Pauline South Carolina 29374
                             https://www.journeymanpublishing.com

Publisher's Note

Across the United States, regions experiencing sustained growth are asking the same question in different ways: how do we welcome new residents and investment without losing the qualities that made these places desirable in the first place? The answers are often debated in terms of individual projects, zoning decisions, or infrastructure constraints. Less often are they framed as a system — one in which housing supply, infrastructure, policy, time, and capital interact to shape long-term outcomes.

This volume contributes to that broader conversation through the lens of Upstate South Carolina. While the examples are regional, the underlying dynamics are not. Communities along and beyond the I-85 corridor are encountering patterns increasingly common across the country: rising demand, pressure on infrastructure, competing expectations for land use, and the challenge of maintaining affordability over time. What distinguishes this work is not that it takes a position on growth, but that it makes the structure of the problem visible.

The Rational High-Growth Management (RHGM) model presented in these pages is offered as a practical framework rather than a prescription. It reflects the idea that successful regions do not rely on any single policy lever. Instead, they manage a balance—between growth and infrastructure, flexibility and predictability, and present needs and long-term outcomes. The case studies illustrate how that balance can be lost, maintained, or restored under different conditions.

Journeyman Publishing is committed to works that translate complex, often fragmented discussions into forms that can be understood, debated, and applied. This volume is intended for policymakers, planners, builders, landowners, and citizens alike—anyone with a stake in how their community grows. If it succeeds, it will not end the conversation, but provide a clearer way to have it.

i

Introduction

The Upstate of South Carolina is entering a period of sustained economic and population growth that will shape the region for generations. Communities across the Greenville–Spartanburg corridor are already experiencing the early signs of that expansion: new housing developments, infrastructure pressure, rising land values, and increasing public debate about how growth should be managed.

This Rational High-Growth Management (RHGM) series examines those issues through real examples from around the country and the Southeast, ultimately proposing a practical vision for how the Upstate—especially Spartanburg County—can become one of the most desirable places in America to live, build a business, and raise a family.

Contents

About SpartansFirst

SpartansFirst advocates that growth strengthens our community rather than straining it. We focus on matching development with the infrastructure we all rely on so families, businesses, and individuals can thrive.

Unlike a traditional chamber of commerce, our nonprofit organization takes a regional view—connecting Spartanburg to surrounding communities and filling the gaps not covered by other organizations. We stand behind and support our law enforcement and first responders, recognizing their vital role in keeping our community safe and prosperous.

We empower innovation and entrepreneurship with education, mentoring, and recognition initiatives and implement innovative technologies addressing accessibility and productivity. SpartansFirst, as an independent volunteer organization, is actively contributing to shape Spartanburg's future to ensure smart, safe, and enduring prosperity for generations to come.

Why the Greenville Concurrency Debate Matters: The Opening Question in Rational Growth Management

Across the Upstate of South Carolina, a quiet but very important conversation has begun. Greenville County leaders have proposed exploring a planning concept known as development concurrency — a policy approach intended to ensure that infrastructure keeps pace with growth. At first glance, the idea sounds straightforward and even obvious: roads, water systems, sewer capacity, schools, and public services should be adequate before new development is approved. Few people would disagree with that principle.

But public policy is rarely as simple as its initial premise. The question facing Greenville, and increasingly the entire Upstate, is not whether growth should be managed. The real question is how it should be managed, and whether the tools chosen will protect the public interest without unintentionally creating new problems. Across the United States, regions that adopted growth-management tools with good intentions have sometimes produced outcomes no one expected: sharply rising housing costs, declining housing supply, increased barriers for small builders, and difficulty for families to find affordable homes.

The Upstate stands at an important moment. Population growth is accelerating, economic investment is increasing, and the Greenville–Spartanburg corridor is becoming one of the most dynamic regions in the Southeast. Decisions made now about how to manage growth will shape the region for decades. Greenville's concurrency discussion is therefore not just a local technical issue. It is the opening chapter of a much larger question: How can the Upstate manage high growth rationally while preserving affordability, opportunity, and quality of life?

Understanding the Principle of Concurrency

In planning terminology, concurrency means that infrastructure must be available at the same time development occurs. If roads, utilities, schools, or other public services are not sufficient to support a proposed development, the project may be delayed until improvements are built or funded.

In theory, the concept is attractive. It reflects a common-sense idea that growth should not outrun the systems that support it. Many communities have experienced the frustration of subdivisions appearing faster than roads can be widened, or new commercial centers arriving before utilities are expanded. Residents understandably ask why development should proceed when infrastructure is already strained.

Concurrency attempts to answer that question by linking development approvals to measurable infrastructure capacity. In practice, it can involve detailed standards such as road traffic thresholds, water and sewer availability, school capacity, emergency service response times, and other indicators of public readiness.

The goal is to ensure that growth occurs in balance with infrastructure , rather than forcing taxpayers to catch up later.

That objective is reasonable. In fact, most citizens would agree that infrastructure planning should be responsible and forward-looking. But concurrency, like many policy tools, can produce unintended effects depending on how it is designed and implemented.

Why Greenville Is Considering Concurrency

Greenville County's interest in concurrency did not appear suddenly. It is the result of several long-term trends that are now converging.

First, the Upstate is experiencing sustained population growth. People continue moving to the region because of its strong economy, quality of life, moderate cost of living, and strategic location along the Interstate 85 corridor. Employers ranging from advanced manufacturers to logistics firms and technology companies have expanded operations across the region.

Second, that growth has placed visible pressure on infrastructure. Residents increasingly report traffic congestion on major corridors, concerns about road capacity, and questions about whether public utilities and schools can keep pace with new development.

Third, there is a growing expectation among citizens that local governments should demonstrate that they are planning responsibly for the future. Public officials understandably want to show that growth is being managed thoughtfully rather than simply reacting to events.

Concurrency appears to offer a structured way to address these concerns. By tying development approvals to infrastructure readiness, county leaders hope to prevent situations in which growth overwhelms roads, utilities, or public services.

The motivation behind the proposal is therefore understandable. Communities want growth that strengthens the region rather than diminishing quality of life.

Why the Idea Sounds So Reasonable

Policies like concurrency often gain early support because they align with basic ideas of fairness and responsibility.

Residents who already live in a community frequently ask why new development should be allowed if roads are already crowded or if public services appear stretched. From that perspective, requiring infrastructure to keep pace with development seems logical.

There is also a widely shared belief that growth should pay for growth. Many citizens worry that taxpayers end up subsidizing development through infrastructure expansions that follow new projects. A concurrency framework can appear to shift that burden toward developers or project sponsors rather than existing residents.

Another appealing feature is predictability. If infrastructure standards are clearly defined, developers may know in advance what conditions must be met for approval. In theory, this could create a more orderly process for planning growth.

These ideas are not inherently wrong. Responsible planning does require attention to infrastructure capacity and public investment. But policies designed around these principles must also consider the broader economic system in which development occurs. The First Warning Signs The most important caution about concurrency is simple: the policy does not create infrastructure by itself.

Concurrency sets conditions under which development may occur, but it does not build roads, expand water plants, or construct schools. If infrastructure improvements take years to plan and finance—as they often do—development approvals may be delayed for long periods even when housing demand remains strong.

Those delays can have significant consequences.

When housing construction slows while population growth continues, the supply of available homes tightens. Builders face uncertainty about whether projects will be approved or postponed. Financing becomes more complicated, smaller developers may withdraw from the market, and projects that do move forward may shift toward higher-end housing in order to absorb rising costs.

The result can be an unintended chain reaction: reduced housing supply leads to higher prices, which make it harder for working families to remain in the community.

In other words, a policy intended to protect residents from the effects of growth can sometimes make the cost of living higher for those same residents if housing availability becomes constrained.

This possibility does not mean concurrency should never be considered. It means the policy must be examined carefully and designed with a full understanding of how housing markets and development economics operate.

Questions That Must Be Asked

Any discussion of concurrency or similar growth-management tools should begin with several fundamental questions.

Who ultimately pays for infrastructure improvements? If developers are required to fund upgrades, those costs may eventually appear in the price of homes or commercial space.

How will delays affect housing supply? Even temporary uncertainty in the approval process can discourage construction, particularly for smaller builders who cannot absorb extended timelines.

How will policies affect landowners? Families who have owned property for generations may depend on development opportunities to realize the value of their land. If approvals become uncertain or delayed indefinitely, those landowners may lose the ability to monetize assets they have maintained for decades.

How will small projects be treated compared to large ones? Complex regulatory systems often favor large developers with substantial financial resources while making it difficult for smaller builders to operate.

How will infrastructure improvements actually be funded and scheduled? Without a realistic plan for financing roads, utilities, and public services, concurrency may simply become a mechanism for postponing development rather than solving infrastructure problems.

These questions are not objections to planning. They are essential components of responsible planning.

The Broader Issue for the Upstate

Although Greenville County initiated the concurrency discussion, the implications extend far beyond one jurisdiction.

The Upstate region functions as a connected economic corridor stretching from Anderson through Greenville and Spartanburg and along Interstate 85 toward Charlotte and Atlanta. Decisions made in one county inevitably affect neighboring communities.

If one county restricts development significantly, housing demand may shift to surrounding counties. Infrastructure pressure can move across county lines. Regional employers depend on workers who can live within reasonable commuting distance of job centers.

For these reasons, the concurrency debate should be viewed as part of a broader regional conversation about how the Upstate intends to manage growth over the coming decades.

The region has many advantages: a strong manufacturing base, growing research institutions, a culture of entrepreneurship, and an attractive quality of life. Maintaining those strengths requires policies that support both infrastructure investment and continued opportunity for families and businesses.

A Moment for Careful Thinking

Growth management is one of the most challenging responsibilities local governments face. Communities want to preserve the qualities that make them desirable while also welcoming new residents, new businesses, and new opportunities.

History shows that well-intentioned policies can produce unexpected results when they are implemented without careful attention to housing supply, economic incentives, and long-term infrastructure planning.

The Greenville concurrency discussion therefore deserves thoughtful examination rather than quick approval or quick dismissal. The principle behind the idea is understandable. But the Upstate must ensure that any approach adopted truly improves the balance between growth and infrastructure without creating new barriers to affordability or opportunity.

The conversation that has begun in Greenville offers a valuable opportunity for the entire region to consider what rational growth management should look like in the decades ahead.

Looking Ahead

The next article in this series will examine a cautionary case from outside the region. California's housing crisis is often discussed in political debates, but the real lesson is more complex than simple slogans. Over time, a combination of housing supply constraints, regulatory delays, and planning fragmentation contributed to dramatic increases in housing costs and rising homelessness.

Understanding what went wrong in California is essential for regions like the Upstate that are now experiencing rapid growth. By studying those mistakes carefully, communities can recognize early warning signs and design policies that protect both infrastructure and housing affordability.

The goal of this series is not to oppose growth or to advocate unrestricted development. The goal is to explore a rational approach to managing high growth—one that preserves opportunity, respects property rights, supports family affordability, and keeps infrastructure aligned with the future of the Upstate. Greenville's concurrency debate is simply the place where that larger conversation begins.

When Growth Management Goes Wrong: California, Housing Scarcity, and the Cost of Policy Failure

In the first article of this series, we examined Greenville County's interest in development concurrency and the broader question facing the Upstate: how to manage growth responsibly while preserving affordability and opportunity. The principle behind concurrency, aligning development with infrastructure, is understandable and often reasonable. But the experience of other regions shows that growth-management policies can produce unintended consequences if they are not carefully designed.

Few places illustrate those consequences more clearly than California. Over several decades, a combination of well-intentioned policies, regulatory complexity, and housing supply constraints contributed to one of the most severe housing affordability crises in the United States. The result has been extraordinarily high housing costs and rising homelessness across many parts of the state.

California's experience should not be reduced to political slogans or oversimplified explanations. It is a complex story involving many variables: economic success, population growth, environmental regulation, local governance structures, and market dynamics. But the core lesson is unmistakable. When housing supply fails to keep pace with demand, and when policy systems make it difficult to build new housing, the cost of living rises dramatically, and the consequences eventually reach the most vulnerable residents.

For rapidly growing regions like the Upstate of South Carolina, California's experience offers a cautionary case. The purpose of examining it is not to criticize another state, but to understand what went wrong and how similar outcomes can be avoided.

The Housing Supply Problem At the center of California's housing crisis is a simple imbalance: demand for housing greatly exceeded the supply of homes being built. California has one of the largest and most productive economies in the world. It hosts major technology industries, research universities, entertainment companies, and global financial networks. These industries attract workers from across the country and around the world.

Yet while employment and population grew steadily, housing construction failed to keep pace. For decades, California built far fewer homes than population growth required. As the supply of available housing tightened, prices rose rapidly.

In competitive housing markets, scarcity produces predictable results. Buyers compete for limited homes. Renters face rising rents as landlords respond to demand. Over time, the gap between incomes and housing costs widens.

What began as a supply imbalance gradually became a structural affordability crisis affecting millions of residents.

Regulatory Complexity and Approval Delays

Housing supply shortages did not occur simply because of population growth. They were compounded by the complexity of California's development approval system.

Many housing projects must navigate multiple layers of local review, environmental analysis, public hearings, and potential litigation before construction can begin. While these processes were originally created to protect environmental resources and give communities a voice in planning decisions, they gradually became increasingly complex and time-consuming.

Developers often face approval timelines that extend for several years before construction begins. During that time, financing costs accumulate, market conditions change, and uncertainty increases.

Large development companies sometimes have the financial capacity to absorb these delays. Smaller builders and local developers often do not. As a result, the number of firms capable of producing housing shrinks, further reducing supply.

When delays become the norm rather than the exception, the housing market begins to operate under structural scarcity.

Local Opposition and Fragmented Governance

Another factor contributing to California's housing shortage is the fragmented nature of local land-use authority.

Cities and counties hold significant control over zoning decisions and development approvals. Residents who oppose new housing projects, often referred to as "Not In My Back Yard," or NIMBY opposition, can exert substantial influence on local decisions.

In many communities, this opposition has led to reductions in housing density, lengthy review processes, or outright rejection of projects that would add new homes.

While local concerns about neighborhood character or traffic impacts are understandable, the cumulative effect across many jurisdictions has been a substantial reduction in the amount of housing that can be built.

Because housing markets operate regionally rather than city by city, decisions made in one jurisdiction often shift demand to another without solving the overall shortage.

The Escalation of Housing Costs

As housing supply tightened across California, the economic consequences became increasingly severe.

Home prices and rents rose to levels far above the national average. In many metropolitan areas, median home prices climbed into the millions of dollars, placing homeownership far beyond the reach of many middle-income families.

Rental markets followed the same pattern. As rents increased, households with moderate incomes began spending a larger share of their earnings on housing. Many families found themselves paying more than half of their income simply to remain housed.

Young adults delayed homeownership or left the state entirely in search of affordable housing. Workers essential to local economies (teachers, police officers, healthcare workers, and service employees) often found it difficult to live near the communities they served.

Housing affordability became one of the defining public policy issues in the state.

The Connection to Homelessness

Rising housing costs do not automatically cause homelessness. Homelessness is influenced by multiple factors including mental health challenges, substance abuse, family instability, and economic hardship.

However, housing affordability plays a crucial role in determining how vulnerable individuals and families respond to those challenges.

When housing costs are relatively moderate, families experiencing temporary financial hardship may still be able to find lower-cost housing or rely on extended family arrangements. But when rents and home prices rise dramatically, the margin of safety disappears.

Households living paycheck to paycheck can be pushed out of housing by even small disruptions: a lost job, a medical emergency, or a sudden rent increase. Without affordable alternatives, some individuals eventually fall into homelessness.

In high-cost housing markets, the number of people living near that financial edge increases significantly.

This dynamic has been observed in many parts of California, where rising housing costs have been one factor contributing to visible increases in homelessness over time.

The Policy Warning Signs

California's experience provides several warning signs that rapidly growing regions should recognize early.

First, housing supply must remain a central priority. Policies that unintentionally reduce the number of homes being built can create long-term affordability problems even if those policies were originally intended to protect communities.

Second, approval processes must remain predictable and efficient. Long delays and uncertainty discourage builders and increase costs for those who remain in the market.

Third, infrastructure policies must be paired with realistic funding strategies. Requirements that development wait for infrastructure improvements can delay housing supply if governments lack the resources to build those improvements quickly.

Fourth, growth management tools should be targeted rather than blanket restrictions. Different areas of a region have different infrastructure capacities, and policies should reflect those differences rather than applying rigid standards everywhere.

Finally, policymakers must recognize that housing affordability is not merely a statistic. Affordability directly affects the stability of families and communities.

The Fairness Question

Another dimension of growth management often receives less attention: fairness to property owners.

Families who have owned land for generations frequently view development as the primary opportunity to realize the value of that asset. If approval processes become uncertain or restrictive, those landowners may find themselves unable to sell or develop property in a reasonable timeframe.

In some cases, policies designed to control growth can unintentionally shift economic burdens onto landowners who have maintained property for decades in anticipation of eventual development opportunities.

Fair policy must therefore consider not only the interests of current residents and future buyers, but also the rights and expectations of property owners whose land forms part of the community's growth.

What the Upstate Can Learn

The Upstate of South Carolina stands in a very different position from California. Housing costs remain relatively moderate compared with many coastal regions, and there is still significant land available for development.

This position offers an advantage: the region has the opportunity to learn from the experiences of others before encountering similar problems.

The key lesson is that growth management should not create artificial scarcity. Policies designed to align infrastructure with development must also preserve the ability to build sufficient housing for the population that the region will inevitably to attract.

Regions that maintain a healthy supply of housing are far less likely to experience the affordability crises that have affected some high-cost metropolitan areas.

Looking Ahead

The purpose of examining California's experience is not to suggest that the Upstate will inevitably face the same challenges. Rather, it highlights the importance of balancing infrastructure planning with housing supply and economic opportunity.

Growth is not the enemy of a thriving community. In many cases, growth reflects economic vitality and the attractiveness of a region to new residents and businesses.

The challenge lies in ensuring that growth occurs in a way that strengthens communities rather than placing pressure on affordability and infrastructure.

The next article in this series will turn from caution to possibility by examining a high-growth region that has taken a different approach. Austin, Texas, has experienced extraordinary population growth in recent years, yet it has pursued policies designed to expand housing supply while coordinating infrastructure and transportation planning.

Austin's experience offers valuable lessons about how rapidly growing regions can adapt to change without sacrificing opportunity or affordability.

Austin's Lesson: Expanding Housing Supply While Managing Rapid Growth

In the previous article we examined California's housing crisis and the long-term consequences of allowing housing supply to fall behind population and job growth. The lesson from California is not simply that growth is difficult to manage, but that policies which restrict housing supply, intentionally or unintentionally, can create powerful economic pressures that eventually raise housing costs and destabilize communities.

Fortunately, California is not the only example available. Other fast-growing regions have faced similar pressures but have responded differently. One of the most interesting examples in recent years is Austin, Texas , a city that experienced extraordinary population growth during the past two decades.

Austin's experience is important because it demonstrates that a rapidly growing region does not have to choose between economic expansion and housing affordability. While Austin still faces challenges, it has taken deliberate steps to expand housing supply, adjust land-use policies, and rethink how infrastructure and transportation interact with development. Those efforts have produced measurable effects in the housing market and offer useful lessons for other regions facing similar growth pressures.

For communities in the Upstate of South Carolina, Austin provides an example of how growth can be accommodated without allowing housing scarcity to dominate the market.

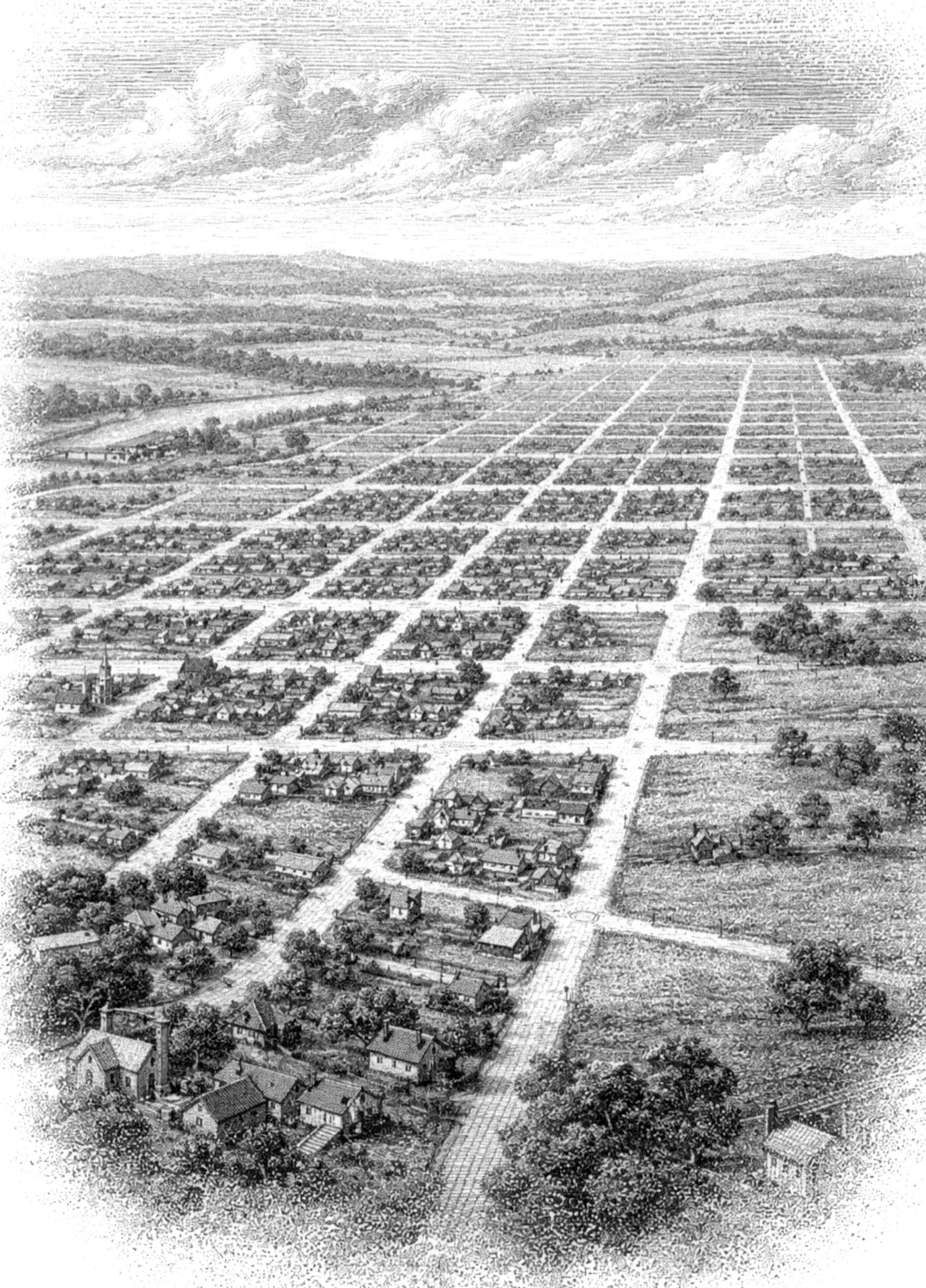

Austin's Rapid Growth

Austin's population growth during the past two decades has been dramatic. The city has become one of the nation's leading centers for technology, innovation, and entrepreneurship. Major employers including semiconductor companies, technology firms, research institutions, and advanced manufacturers have expanded in the region.

The metropolitan area's economic momentum has attracted workers from across the United States. New residents arrive seeking employment opportunities, a vibrant cultural environment, and a relatively moderate cost of living compared with coastal technology centers.

As a result, Austin's population increased rapidly. The metropolitan region added hundreds of thousands of residents in a relatively short period of time. Housing demand surged as workers relocated to the area and local incomes rose.

This situation could easily have produced the same type of housing scarcity that developed in parts of California. Instead, Austin began exploring ways to expand the housing supply while coordinating infrastructure improvements.

The Importance of Housing Supply

One of the most important principles underlying Austin's approach is recognition that housing supply plays a central role in determining housing costs.

When new residents move into a region faster than homes are built, the supply of available housing tightens. Buyers compete for limited properties, rents rise, and developers face pressure to focus on higher-end projects that can absorb rising costs.

Austin's leaders recognized that allowing housing supply to stagnate would eventually lead to the same affordability problems that other fast-growing regions experienced.

Instead, the city began examining ways to allow more homes to be built within existing neighborhoods and along transportation corridors.

This approach did not eliminate all housing cost pressures, but it helped maintain a level of supply that prevented the market from becoming severely constrained.

Expanding Housing Options

One of the most significant steps Austin took involved reforming zoning and land-use rules that had historically limited housing density in many areas of the city.

For decades, large portions of the city permitted only single-family homes on individual lots. While that pattern had once been appropriate for a smaller city, it limited the number of homes that could be built as Austin grew.

To address this challenge, the city adopted reforms that allowed multiple housing units on lots that previously allowed only one home. These changes created opportunities for duplexes, small multifamily buildings, and other housing forms that increase the number of available homes without dramatically altering neighborhood character.

By expanding the range of housing types, Austin opened the door for additional supply to enter the market. Smaller homes, townhouses, and accessory dwelling units began appearing in areas that previously had limited housing options.

The goal was not to eliminate single-family neighborhoods but to create more flexibility in how land could be used , allowing the housing market to respond to population growth.

The Role of Transportation

Planning Another important element of Austin's strategy involves transportation planning. Rapid growth often produces traffic congestion, and communities frequently attempt to address that congestion by widening roads.

Austin recognized that road expansion alone cannot solve long-term mobility challenges in growing metropolitan areas. Instead, the city began emphasizing a broader approach that includes transit options, transportation demand management, and land-use planning that reduces the distance between homes, workplaces, and services.

By encouraging housing development near employment centers and transportation corridors, Austin aims to reduce the need for long daily commutes. Mixed-use development, where housing, retail, and offices exist in close proximity, also helps shorten travel distances.

This integrated approach recognizes that housing policy and transportation policy are closely connected. If housing is located far from employment centers, infrastructure costs increase and congestion becomes more difficult to manage.

Infrastructure as a System

Austin's growth strategy also reflects a broader understanding of infrastructure. Roads, utilities, schools, parks, and public services are not isolated systems. They interact with each other and must be planned in a way that is interdependent.

Rather than relying exclusively on project-by-project infrastructure requirements, the city has emphasized longer-term planning through capital improvement programs and regional coordination. These programs identify areas where infrastructure expansion will be needed and establish funding priorities to support growth.

This approach allows infrastructure investments to anticipate development rather than merely reacting to it. By aligning infrastructure planning with expected growth patterns, Austin seeks to maintain capacity while avoiding the delays that can occur when infrastructure improvements lag behind development approvals.

Measurable Effects in the Housing Market

One of the most interesting developments in Austin's housing market occurred in recent years when a wave of new housing construction entered the market.

As additional apartments and homes were completed, rental price increases began to slow and in some cases declined. While housing affordability remains an ongoing challenge, the increase in supply helped reduce the upward pressure on rents that had previously been accelerating.

This outcome illustrates a key economic principle: when supply increases, price pressure can ease. The effect may not eliminate affordability concerns entirely, but it can prevent housing markets from becoming severely constrained.

For rapidly growing regions, maintaining a steady flow of housing construction is therefore one of the most effective ways to keep housing accessible to a broad range of residents.

What Austin Has Not Solved

Austin's experience is not a perfect success story. Like many growing cities, it continues to face challenges.

Housing prices remain higher than they were a decade ago. Population growth continues to place pressure on infrastructure systems. Neighborhood debates over zoning changes can be intense, and implementing transportation improvements requires significant investment and time.

In addition, expanding housing supply alone cannot solve every affordability issue. Wage levels, construction costs, and land prices all influence the housing market.

Nevertheless, Austin's policies demonstrate that cities can respond to growth proactively rather than allowing housing shortages to develop. Lessons for the Upstate For the Upstate of South Carolina, Austin's experience offers several important lessons.

First, housing supply should be viewed as an essential component of growth management. Regions that maintain a steady supply of new housing are less likely to experience extreme affordability crises.

Second, flexibility in housing types can expand opportunities for both builders and residents. Allowing a wider range of housing forms enables the market to respond more effectively to changing population needs.

Third, transportation planning and land-use planning must work together. Locating housing near employment centers and major transportation corridors can reduce infrastructure costs and improve mobility.

Fourth, infrastructure planning should anticipate growth rather than react to it. Long-term capital improvement strategies can help ensure that utilities, roads, and public services keep pace with development.

Finally, growth management should focus on coordination rather than restriction. Policies designed to organize development often produce better outcomes than policies that simply attempt to limit it.

Looking Ahead

Austin's experience shows that rapid growth does not have to lead inevitably to housing scarcity or economic strain. With thoughtful policy adjustments and coordinated infrastructure planning, communities can accommodate growth while maintaining opportunities for new residents and existing families.

The next article in this series will expand the discussion by examining two additional regions that have developed distinct approaches to growth management. Northern Virginia has demonstrated the power of regional transportation planning and corridor-based development, while Florida offers decades of experience with tools such as concurrency, impact fees, and infrastructure credits.

Together, these examples will illustrate how different policy tools can be combined to align infrastructure with development while preserving the housing supply necessary for thriving communities.

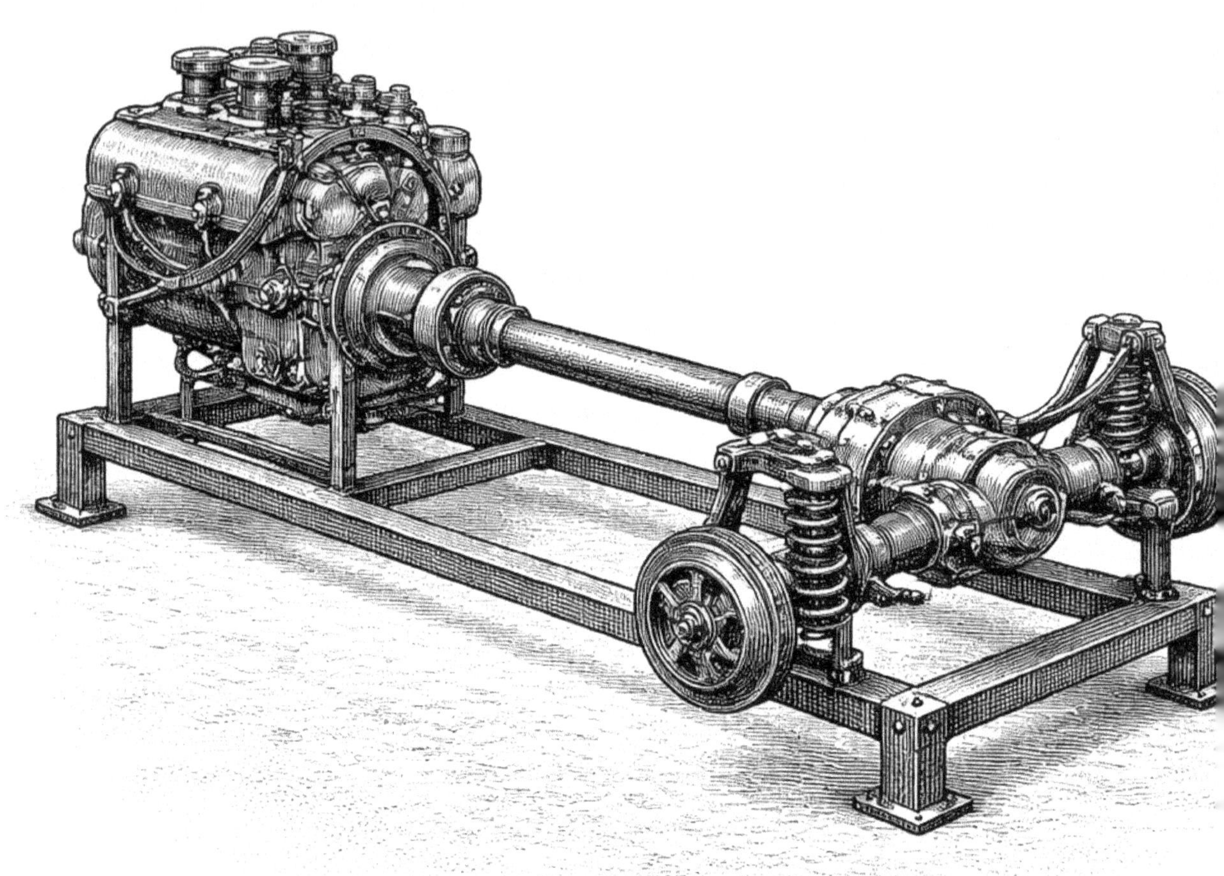

Best Practices and Caution Flags: What Northern Virginia and Florida Teach About Aligning Growth With Infrastructure

The first three articles in this series examined the opening policy discussion in Greenville County, the cautionary experience of California's housing shortage, and the example of Austin's efforts to expand housing supply while coordinating infrastructure and transportation planning. These cases illustrate both the risks and the opportunities that accompany rapid population growth.

But no single city or state offers a perfect model. Communities that manage growth effectively usually rely on a combination of planning strategies, infrastructure financing tools, and housing policies rather than a single regulatory approach.

Two regions that offer particularly useful lessons are Northern Virginia and Florida. Both have experienced sustained population growth and have developed planning tools designed to align infrastructure with development. Their successes, and their mistakes, demonstrate how growth management can either support thriving communities or unintentionally restrict housing supply and economic opportunity.

The experiences of these regions illustrate a central principle: effective growth management requires flexible systems and careful calibration, not rigid restrictions that ignore housing supply and market realities.

Northern Virginia: Regional Coordination in a High-Growth Economy

Northern Virginia sits just across the Potomac River from Washington, D.C., and has become one of the most economically dynamic regions in the United States. Counties such as Arlington, Fairfax, Loudoun, and Prince William have experienced steady population growth for decades, driven by federal government employment, defense contracting, technology companies, and professional services.

Managing growth in this environment required planning at a regional scale. Rather than allowing each county to operate independently, Northern Virginia developed organizations capable of coordinating transportation and infrastructure planning across the region.

One of the most important institutions involved in this effort is the Northern Virginia Transportation Authority (NVTA). NVTA helps fund and prioritize major transportation investments that serve multiple jurisdictions. By coordinating projects across counties, the region has been able to align road improvements, transit expansions, and development planning more effectively than if each county acted alone.

This regional coordination helps ensure that infrastructure investments support long-term growth rather than reacting to individual development proposals in isolation. Arlington County and the Rosslyn–Ballston Corridor One of the most frequently cited examples of successful corridor-based planning in the United States is located in Arlington County, Virginia along the Rosslyn–Ballston corridor.

During the 1970s and 1980s, Arlington faced a major planning decision as the Washington Metro rail system expanded through the county. Instead of allowing development to spread evenly across residential neighborhoods, county leaders concentrated higher-density development around five Metro stations: Rosslyn, Courthouse, Clarendon, Virginia Square, and Ballston.

Office towers, apartments, restaurants, and retail spaces were built within walking distance of the stations, creating a series of mixed-use urban centers connected by rail transit. Meanwhile, nearby residential neighborhoods remained largely intact.

This strategy allowed Arlington to support significant population and employment growth while minimizing disruption to established neighborhoods.

It also reduced the need for long automobile commutes, because residents could live near transit and jobs.

The Rosslyn–Ballston corridor remains one of the clearest demonstrations of how concentrated development around transportation infrastructure can support both economic growth and livable communities. Fairfax County and the Richmond Highway Corridor Another instructive example in Northern Virginia is Fairfax County's redevelopment strategy along Richmond Highway (U.S. Route 1).

For decades the corridor consisted primarily of aging strip commercial development and low-density suburban housing. Recognizing the corridor's proximity to Washington, D.C., and the need for more housing options, Fairfax County adopted plans to transform the area into a series of mixed-use activity centers.

The county introduced bus rapid transit planning , higher-density zoning near key intersections, and redevelopment incentives designed to attract new residential and commercial projects.

By focusing development in defined centers along the corridor, Fairfax County aims to increase housing supply while improving transportation options and revitalizing older commercial areas.

This approach demonstrates how corridor planning can guide redevelopment rather than allowing scattered, inefficient expansion.

Florida's Long Experience with Concurrency

Florida provides another important set of lessons. The state has experienced continuous population growth for many decades as people moved south for employment, retirement, and climate. Managing this growth required planning systems capable of aligning development with infrastructure.

Florida became known for its use of development concurrency , a policy framework requiring that public facilities be adequate to support new development at the time that development occurs.

One of the earliest and most influential examples of concurrency implementation occurred in Broward County , part of the Miami–Fort Lauderdale metropolitan area.

During the 1980s and 1990s, Broward adopted concurrency standards designed to ensure that roads, schools, and utilities were capable of supporting new development before approvals were granted.

The policy helped prevent some forms of infrastructure overload but also revealed the challenges of rigid concurrency standards when growth pressures remained strong.

Miami-Dade County and Mobility Fees

Another example comes from Miami-Dade County, which developed a mobility fee system to help fund transportation improvements associated with development.

Instead of relying solely on traditional road capacity measurements, Miami-Dade began exploring ways to fund multimodal transportation systems, including transit, pedestrian infrastructure, and roadway improvements, through fees paid by new development.

The goal was to ensure that growth contributed to transportation infrastructure while allowing flexibility in how mobility improvements were delivered.

Miami-Dade also introduced exemptions and adjustments for certain affordable housing developments, recognizing that infrastructure fees can raise housing costs if applied uniformly across all projects.

Osceola County and Workforce Housing Fee Relief

In central Florida, Osceola County , located south of Orlando, has adopted a policy approach that combines impact fees with incentives for workforce housing.

Rapid population growth in the Orlando metropolitan region created strong demand for new housing. Osceola County implemented impact fees to support infrastructure expansion but later recognized that these fees could make workforce housing projects financially difficult.

To address this challenge, the county established a Mobility Fee Relief Program that reduces fees for developments providing affordable or workforce housing units.

This policy reflects a growing understanding among planners that infrastructure financing systems must be carefully calibrated to avoid discouraging the types of housing most needed by local workers.

Indian River County and Flexible Concurrency

A final example comes from Indian River County on Florida's east coast. The county continues to operate under concurrency requirements but has implemented procedures that allow developers to reserve infrastructure capacity early in the approval process.

This approach helps prevent projects from being delayed indefinitely while infrastructure improvements are planned. By providing clearer pathways for compliance, the county has been able to maintain concurrency standards without halting housing development.

Indian River's experience illustrates how concurrency systems can evolve toward greater flexibility while still protecting infrastructure capacity.

Lessons From Northern Virginia and Florida

Taken together, the experiences of Northern Virginia and Florida reveal several important principles.

First, regional coordination is often essential. Infrastructure systems, particularly transportation networks, cross jurisdictional boundaries, making collaboration among counties and cities critical.

Second, corridor-based planning can organize growth efficiently. Concentrating development along transportation corridors allows infrastructure investments to serve larger populations without expanding costs across every neighborhood.

Third, impact fees and mobility fees can provide funding for infrastructure, but they must be carefully calibrated so that they do not raise housing costs excessively.

Fourth, flexibility is critical. Policies that include credits, exemptions, or alternative compliance mechanisms allow communities to encourage housing supply while maintaining infrastructure standards.

Finally, rigidity can create unintended consequences. Concurrency systems that rely exclusively on road capacity standards or delay development indefinitely can inadvertently restrict housing supply and increase prices.

Implications for the Upstate

The Upstate of South Carolina is not identical to Northern Virginia or Florida, but the region shares some of their characteristics. Population growth along the Interstate 85 corridor connects Greenville, Spartanburg, and surrounding communities in an expanding regional economy.

These conditions suggest that the Upstate may benefit from combining several planning strategies: corridor-based development, flexible infrastructure financing tools, and regional coordination across counties.

At the same time, policymakers must remain mindful of housing supply. Infrastructure policies should not unintentionally reduce the availability of homes needed by families moving into the region.

Looking Ahead

Northern Virginia and Florida demonstrate that growth management is rarely solved through a single policy. Instead, communities must balance infrastructure planning, housing supply, economic development, and long-term regional coordination.

The next article in this series will examine a case study much closer to home. Gwinnett County, Georgia , located northeast of Atlanta along Interstate 85, experienced one of the most dramatic suburban growth transformations in the Southeast.

Gwinnett's transition from a rural county to a major metropolitan community provides a regional example of how rapid growth unfolds over time—and how planning strategies evolve as communities adapt to new realities.

Gwinnett County, Georgia: A Southeastern Growth Laboratory and What the Upstate Can Learn

Throughout this series we have examined several examples of how regions respond to rapid population growth. California showed the dangers of housing scarcity and regulatory complexity. Austin illustrated how expanding housing supply can moderate price pressure even during economic expansion. Northern Virginia and Florida demonstrated how corridor planning, infrastructure financing, and concurrency systems can help align development with public capacity.

Yet there is another example that may be even more relevant to the Upstate of South Carolina: Gwinnett County, Georgia.

Located northeast of Atlanta along the Interstate 85 corridor, Gwinnett experienced one of the most dramatic suburban growth transformations in the modern American South. Within a single generation it changed from a largely rural county into one of the most populous counties in Georgia and a major economic center within the Atlanta metropolitan region.

Gwinnett's story is not simply a tale of rapid expansion. It is also a case study in how communities respond to the pressures created by growth. The county faced many of the same challenges now appearing in parts of the Upstate: traffic congestion, suburban sprawl, infrastructure strain, and the need to adapt planning systems as population increased.

Because Gwinnett's experience unfolded over several decades, it provides a valuable regional example of how growth patterns evolve—and how planning strategies must evolve with them.

From Rural County to Metropolitan Suburb

For most of its early history, Gwinnett County was primarily rural. Farms, small towns, and scattered communities defined the landscape. That began to change after the construction of Interstate 85 , which connected the county directly to Atlanta.

The interstate highway made commuting between Gwinnett and Atlanta far easier. As the Atlanta economy expanded during the late twentieth century, housing demand spread outward into surrounding counties where land was still available.

Gwinnett quickly became one of the most attractive locations for suburban development. Developers built large residential subdivisions, shopping centers, and business parks. Families moved into the county seeking affordable housing and access to employment opportunities in Atlanta.

The population growth that followed was extraordinary.

In 1970 Gwinnett had fewer than 75,000 residents. By 1990 the population had surpassed 350,000. By 2010 the county had grown to more than 800,000 residents, making it one of the fastest-growing counties in the United States during that period.

This expansion fundamentally transformed the county's character. What had once been farmland and small towns became a dense suburban landscape connected to one of the nation's largest metropolitan areas.

The Early Growth Pattern: Suburban Expansion

Like many rapidly growing counties during the late twentieth century, Gwinnett's early development followed the classic suburban pattern.

Large subdivisions spread across previously rural land. Retail development appeared along major roads in the form of shopping centers and strip commercial corridors. Office parks and industrial facilities followed transportation routes that connected the county to Atlanta.

This pattern provided housing quickly and supported economic growth, but it also produced challenges.

Road networks designed for rural traffic suddenly carried thousands of commuters. Infrastructure investments struggled to keep pace with development. Residents increasingly faced longer travel times as congestion appeared on major corridors.

Schools, public safety facilities, parks, and utilities had to expand rapidly to support the growing population.

These pressures forced local leaders to reconsider how development should be organized.

The Infrastructure Challenge

Rapid population growth places significant demands on public infrastructure. Roads must be widened or extended. Water and sewer systems require expansion. New schools and fire stations must be built to serve expanding neighborhoods.

Gwinnett County responded with substantial investments in infrastructure, particularly in transportation.

Major arterial roads were widened to accommodate increasing traffic volumes. Interchanges along Interstate 85 were expanded to support commuter flows and freight transportation. The county invested heavily in water and sewer systems to ensure that new subdivisions and commercial projects could be served reliably.

At the same time, Gwinnett introduced impact fees to help finance infrastructure improvements associated with new development. These fees required developers to contribute to the cost of roads, parks, libraries, and public safety facilities needed to serve growing communities.

Impact fees did not eliminate infrastructure challenges, but they provided a funding mechanism that connected growth with public investment.

The Shift Toward Planning and Coordination

As Gwinnett matured, county leaders recognized that growth could not continue indefinitely without a more coordinated planning framework.

Comprehensive planning became an increasingly important tool. The county developed long-term land-use plans identifying areas appropriate for residential growth, commercial development, and employment centers.

Rather than allowing development to spread evenly across the landscape, planners began encouraging more organized growth patterns.

These efforts included improvements to zoning regulations, stronger development review processes, and expanded capital improvement planning for infrastructure investments.

The goal was not to stop growth but to guide it in ways that reduced infrastructure strain and improved community design.

Activity Centers and Corridor Development

One of the most important planning concepts Gwinnett adopted was the idea of activity centers.

Instead of relying entirely on scattered suburban development, the county identified key intersections and commercial districts where higher-density mixed-use development could occur. These activity centers often included housing, retail, offices, and civic spaces within relatively compact areas.

Examples include the Gwinnett Place area near Duluth , which evolved from a regional shopping mall into a broader redevelopment district with mixed-use potential.

Activity centers allow infrastructure investments to serve larger numbers of people within defined areas rather than extending services across the entire county.

In addition to activity centers, Gwinnett began focusing on major transportation corridors as organizing elements for growth. Development along Interstate 85 and other major routes became more structured, with employment centers, residential communities, and commercial areas linked by transportation infrastructure.

This approach helped create a more coherent development pattern as the county transitioned from rural expansion to mature suburban growth.

Redevelopment and the Suburban Lifecycle

Another challenge that emerged as Gwinnett matured was the aging of earlier suburban development.

Retail centers built during the 1980s and 1990s eventually required reinvestment. Some commercial areas experienced declining activity as shopping patterns changed and newer developments appeared elsewhere.

Recognizing this cycle, Gwinnett began exploring strategies for redevelopment and revitalization.

Older commercial districts were targeted for reinvestment through zoning adjustments, infrastructure improvements, and public-private partnerships. Redevelopment efforts aimed to introduce mixed-use development, housing, and public spaces into areas that had previously been dominated by single-purpose retail centers.

This shift reflects a common pattern in suburban regions: as communities mature, redevelopment becomes as important as new development.

What Gwinnett Did Well

Gwinnett's growth experience produced several positive outcomes.

First, the county allowed substantial housing supply expansion during its growth years. Large numbers of homes were built, helping accommodate population growth and maintain relatively accessible housing opportunities compared with many coastal metropolitan areas.

Second, Gwinnett attracted major employers and developed a diversified economy. Corporate offices, logistics facilities, and advanced manufacturing operations created jobs that supported the region's prosperity.

Third, the county invested heavily in public infrastructure. Roads, utilities, schools, and parks expanded dramatically as the population increased.

Finally, Gwinnett demonstrated an ability to adapt planning strategies over time. As growth patterns evolved, the county adjusted its planning framework to incorporate activity centers, redevelopment strategies, and corridor planning.

Challenges That Took Decades to Address

Despite these successes, Gwinnett's experience also revealed several long-term challenges.

Traffic congestion became a persistent issue as suburban development increased commuting demand. Retrofitting transportation infrastructure after development occurred proved expensive and time-consuming.

Low-density development patterns created infrastructure costs that were higher than they might have been with more concentrated growth.

Public services such as schools required continual expansion to keep pace with population growth.

These challenges illustrate an important lesson: it is far easier to guide growth patterns early than to retrofit infrastructure later.

A Comparison With Spartanburg County

Gwinnett's experience becomes even more interesting when compared with conditions in Spartanburg County.

Gwinnett County today has a land area of about 431 square miles and a population of roughly one million residents.

Spartanburg County, by contrast, has a land area of approximately 807 square miles, nearly twice the size of Gwinnett, but a population of about 370,000 residents.

This comparison highlights an important reality. Spartanburg County still has substantial room for growth compared with Gwinnett's current population density.

The Upstate therefore has an opportunity that Gwinnett did not fully possess during its early growth years: the chance to learn from the experiences of nearby regions before infrastructure pressures reach the same intensity.

By planning thoughtfully today, Spartanburg can guide development patterns that support both economic growth and community livability.

Lessons for the Upstate

Gwinnett County's history offers several lessons for the Upstate.

Growth is easier to guide early than to correct later. Once development patterns are established, retrofitting infrastructure becomes costly and complex.

Housing supply should remain strong. Regions that continue building homes are less likely to experience the extreme affordability crises seen in some other metropolitan areas.

Corridor planning and activity centers can help organize development efficiently. Concentrating growth where infrastructure can support it reduces long-term costs.

Infrastructure investment must anticipate growth rather than react to it.

Finally, long-time landowners should have opportunities to benefit from development without overwhelming public infrastructure systems.

Looking Ahead

Gwinnett County's transformation demonstrates both the opportunities and the challenges that accompany rapid growth in the American South.

The Upstate of South Carolina is now entering a similar phase of expansion as population growth, economic investment, and regional connectivity accelerate along the Interstate 85 corridor.

Understanding how Gwinnett evolved helps illuminate the choices now facing communities in the Upstate.

The final article in this series will bring together the question sparked by Greenville, and the lessons offered by California, Austin, Northern Virginia, Florida, and Gwinnett to outline a forward-looking vision for Spartanburg County and the Upstate region —a vision in which growth strengthens communities, supports families, and makes the region one of the most desirable places in America to live, work, build a business, and raise a family.

A Vision for Upstate South Carolina and Spartanburg County: Becoming the Most Desirable Place in America to Live, Build, Work, and Raise a Family

Throughout this series, we have examined a sequence of real issues and real examples. We began with the concurrency discussion in Greenville County and the larger policy question it raises for the Upstate. We then looked at California as a warning case, showing how housing scarcity, delay, and fragmented policy can slowly produce very high housing costs and rising homelessness. We examined Austin as an example of a high-growth region that recognized the importance of housing supply and flexibility. We looked at Northern Virginia and Florida for practical tools involving corridor planning, regional coordination, impact fees, concurrency, credits, and targeted relief. Then we turned to Gwinnett County, Georgia, a Southeastern case that may be one of the most relevant examples for the Upstate because it shows how a nearby suburban county grew rapidly, prospered, encountered major strain, and then had to evolve its planning model over time.

Now the series comes to its final and most important question: What should Upstate South Carolina do? The answer should not be to fear growth. Growth is not the enemy. Population growth usually means that people and businesses see a region as attractive, promising, and full of opportunity. Nor should the answer be to allow scattered, unstructured development to outrun roads, water, sewer, schools, and public services. That approach produces congestion, inefficiency, public frustration, and expensive retrofits later. The correct answer is a rational middle path: welcome growth, organize it intelligently, preserve affordability, respect property rights, and keep infrastructure aligned with development in a practical and fair way.

That is the vision this final article proposes for Spartanburg County and the broader Upstate.

The Upstate begins this conversation from a position of strength. It already has major advantages that many parts of the country would like to have. It sits along one of the most important economic corridors in the Southeast. It has a strong manufacturing base, logistics strength, access to interstate highways, proximity to Charlotte and Atlanta, and connections to research, technical education, and entrepreneurial activity. It still offers a quality of life that many families find attractive. It remains more affordable than many high-growth regions in the country. It has room to grow. It has a culture of community, work, and family that remains a major asset. In Spartanburg County in particular, the region still has time to make wise choices before the pressures become extreme.

That last point matters. Spartanburg County has far more room than many high-growth counties had by the time they recognized what was happening. Gwinnett County today has a population of about one million residents on roughly 431 square miles of land. Spartanburg County has about 370,000 residents on roughly 807 square miles. That does not mean Spartanburg should seek Gwinnett's density or pattern. It means Spartanburg still has strategic freedom. It can shape growth before the region reaches the level of stress that makes every decision reactive. It can learn from other places rather than repeating their mistakes.

A rational long-range vision for the Upstate should begin with a clear principle: the region should remain a place where ordinary families can still build a life. That sounds simple, but it immediately clarifies the policy direction. A region that wants to remain desirable must keep housing attainable enough for working people, not just high-income households. It must remain a place where a young family can buy or rent a decent home without being crushed by price escalation. It must remain a place where employees can live within reasonable distance of their work. It must remain a place where employers can expand because labor is available and nearby. It must remain a place where older residents, retirees, and long-time citizens are not pushed aside by uncontrolled cost increases.

That means the Upstate should reject one of the most damaging habits seen in other parts of the country: artificial scarcity. When a community makes it too difficult, uncertain, or expensive to build housing, the result is not stability. The result is a restricted supply of homes, escalating prices, and eventually a region that works well for people who already own property but poorly for younger families, new workers, and moderate-income households. That is not a sustainable success model. A prosperous region cannot remain desirable if it quietly turns into a place where ordinary people can no longer afford to live.

The first pillar of the vision should be this: MKaintain abundant housing opportunity. That does not mean careless sprawl. It does not mean approving everything everywhere with no discipline. It means ensuring that the total supply of developable land, housing types, and housing approvals remains broad enough that the market does not become choked by scarcity. Single-family homes, townhouses, smaller detached homes, infill housing, mixed-use residential projects, and well-planned multifamily housing should all have a place within a rational growth model. If a county wants to preserve affordability, it must preserve supply.

The second pillar should be intelligent corridor and activity-center planning. This may be the most practical organizing concept for the Upstate. The region already grows along identifiable corridors, especially Interstate 85, Interstate 26, U.S. 29, and the major routes that connect employment centers, municipalities, and suburban growth areas. Rather than treating all land as though it should grow at the same pace and in the same way, local governments should identify where infrastructure can be expanded efficiently and where higher-intensity growth makes the most sense. Those locations can become activity centers and corridor-based development zones where housing, commerce, offices, and services can be concentrated more intelligently.

This idea is not anti-rural and it is not anti-suburban. In fact, it helps protect both. By steering more intense growth toward selected corridors, interchanges, town centers, and redevelopment districts, a county can reduce the pressure to scatter higher-intensity projects across every part of the landscape. That helps preserve lower-density areas where residents want to maintain a different character. It also reduces the cost of infrastructure because roads, sewer extensions, public services, and other investments can be focused where they generate the most public value.

The third pillar should be measured infrastructure discipline, not rigid anti-growth control. Growth should not simply overwhelm the public. Large developments, high-impact projects, and major growth corridors should carry a fair share of the infrastructure burden they create. Roads, water systems, sewer capacity, drainage, and public safety needs should be evaluated honestly.

The county should be very careful not to create a system so rigid that it effectively becomes a housing choke point. Strict concurrency without an aggressive path to add capacity can become a disguised moratorium. Impact fees set too high can become a hidden housing tax. Long delays can quietly price out small builders and moderate-income projects.

The better model is proportionate and practical. Require major projects to contribute to clearly measurable infrastructure costs. Give full credits when the developer directly builds or funds those improvements. Use phased approvals where appropriate so that infrastructure and development can advance in sequence rather than forcing a complete stop. Distinguish between very large projects and ordinary local-scale development. The objective should be to align growth with infrastructure, not to turn infrastructure policy into a weapon against growth itself.

The fourth pillar should be fairness to long-time landowners and families who own property. This issue is too often ignored in planning debates. A family may have held land for decades or generations. They may have paid taxes, maintained the property, and waited for the day when growth would make that land more valuable. It is not fair to discuss growth entirely from the standpoint of current neighbors and public agencies while treating the landowner's interest as secondary or suspect. Good policy must recognize that these families have legitimate expectations too.

That does not mean every property should immediately become an intense development site. It means the planning system should be predictable enough that owners can reasonably understand the path to realizing value from their land. It means the county should avoid arbitrary delay and constantly shifting standards. It means the county should not trap owners in years of uncertainty while public officials debate growth in abstract terms. Property rights are part of a healthy regional economy, and a rational growth model should respect them openly.

The fifth pillar should be predictability and speed in approvals. One of the clearest lessons from California and from many overregulated regions is that delay is not neutral. Delay is a cost. Delay changes what gets built. Delay favors large developers over smaller builders. Delay increases the chance that only expensive projects can survive the process. A region that wants to remain affordable should aim for clear, understandable, and timely approvals, especially for projects that fit adopted plans and infrastructure expectations.

Predictability also benefits the public. When the rules are clear, residents know what to expect. Developers know where growth belongs and under what terms. Builders can price projects more accurately. Landowners can make rational decisions. Local governments can spend less time fighting repetitive project-by-project battles. A region that wants to become the most desirable place in America to live and work should not be known for confusion, arbitrary delay, and shifting standards. It should be known for being serious, disciplined, and clear.

The sixth pillar should be housing affordability as a strategic economic asset. Too often affordability is treated as a social issue separate from economic development. That is a mistake. Housing affordability is a competitive advantage. A region where workers can still live near their jobs will have an advantage over regions where employers constantly struggle because labor cannot afford to live locally. A region where young families can afford a first home will attract and retain talent. A region where retirees, service workers, technicians, teachers, healthcare employees, and entrepreneurs can all live within the same broad community has a more stable civic structure than one that divides sharply by income and geography.

For Spartanburg County and the Upstate, this means affordability should not be an afterthought added after a crisis appears. It should be designed into growth policy from the beginning. Workforce housing, entry-level housing, moderate-density residential options, and redevelopment with housing components should all be part of the region's planning framework. If infrastructure fees or concurrency-type rules are used, there should be calibrated relief, credits, or faster processing where workforce and family housing is being created in appropriate places.

The seventh pillar should be regional thinking. The Upstate economy does not stop at a county line. Greenville, Spartanburg, Anderson, Cherokee, Pickens, Laurens, and nearby counties are connected by labor markets, transportation corridors, utility systems, and shared economic momentum. One county can shift pressure into another if policy becomes too restrictive or too uncoordinated. Housing, transportation, and infrastructure should therefore be understood regionally even when decisions are made locally.

This does not require a heavy-handed regional bureaucracy. It does require communication, comparative analysis, and recognition that major growth corridors and major infrastructure questions have cross-county effects. If one jurisdiction becomes known for delay and restricted housing supply, some of that growth will spill elsewhere.

If one area fails to plan road or utility capacity, neighboring areas may absorb the side effects. A rational Upstate vision should treat the region as a connected system while allowing each county and municipality to preserve its own character.

The eighth pillar should be redevelopment as well as new development. A mature and desirable region does not only expand outward. It also improves and reuses what it already has. Older commercial centers, underused properties, declining retail corridors, and obsolete industrial sites can often be repositioned into more valuable mixed-use or employment-supporting assets. Redevelopment reduces pressure to extend infrastructure endlessly into new territory. It can also create stronger places by bringing housing, commerce, and public activity into areas that already have road access and utility service.

This matters for Spartanburg County because the county's future should not be imagined only in terms of outward subdivision growth. A national model for rational high-growth management would include strategic redevelopment, better use of existing corridors, revitalization of underperforming sites, and mixed-use opportunities near transportation and employment nodes. That is how a region grows stronger rather than simply larger.

The ninth pillar should be family-centered quality of life. The title of this article speaks deliberately about becoming the most desirable place in America to live, build, work, and raise a family. Those are not separate goals. A county that is easy to do business in but difficult to raise a family in is not fully successful. A county with attractive neighborhoods but weak employment opportunity is not fully successful. A county with growth but declining livability is not fully successful.

Quality of life includes roads that function, neighborhoods that feel stable, good schools, access to healthcare, clean utilities, safe communities, parks and recreation, and housing that people can actually attain. It also includes something harder to measure but just as real: confidence that the community is being managed with common sense and fairness. People want to live in places where growth feels like progress, not like chaos.

The tenth pillar should be leadership that is practical rather than ideological. Some communities become trapped in two bad choices: pure anti-growth politics or pure growth-at-any-cost boosterism. Neither is adequate. The Upstate needs a more mature approach. Leaders should be willing to say yes to growth while also insisting on discipline, planning, and proportionate infrastructure responsibility. They should be willing to protect housing opportunity while refusing to let public systems be overloaded.

They should be willing to support landowners, families, employers, and citizens at the same time.

That kind of leadership is possible because the Upstate still has the conditions needed for it. It is not yet boxed into the crisis posture of some high-cost regions. It is not yet forced to retrofit decades of failed policy with almost no room left to maneuver. It still has land, momentum, affordability advantages, and time to choose wisely.

So what would success look like if the Upstate followed this vision?

It would look like a region where major growth corridors are planned intentionally instead of filling up chaotically. It would look like Spartanburg County identifying strategic activity centers where higher-intensity mixed growth can be served efficiently by roads, water, sewer, and public services. It would look like broad housing opportunity preserved across the county so that families at different income levels still have choices. It would look like infrastructure conditions applied in a measured and predictable way, with credits for direct improvements and relief where needed to preserve workforce housing. It would look like long-time landowners treated as legitimate stakeholders rather than obstacles. It would look like older commercial areas being redeveloped intelligently rather than simply abandoned as growth leaps outward. It would look like counties and municipalities paying attention to one another's decisions rather than pretending each acts in isolation.

Most importantly, it would look like a region that remains open to ordinary ambition. A young couple could buy a first home. A family business could expand. A manufacturer could add workers who can actually afford to live nearby. A landowner could finally realize the value of inherited property. A retired couple could remain in the community. A startup founder could build a company in a place where cost and quality of life still make sense together. That is what it means to become one of the most desirable places in America to live, build, work, and raise a family.

The Upstate should aim higher than merely avoiding mistakes. It should aim to become a national example of how to manage high growth intelligently.

- Not by copying California's restrictions.
- Not by blindly adopting every growth-control mechanism that sounds responsible.
- Not by allowing uncontrolled sprawl to dictate the future.

Build a model based on supply, fairness, predictability, corridor planning, family affordability, and practical infrastructure alignment.

Spartanburg County, in particular, is positioned to lead. It still has enough land, enough flexibility, and enough opportunity to prove that growth can strengthen rather than weaken a community. It can show that property rights and public responsibility do not have to be enemies. It can show that housing affordability is not a secondary issue but a core competitive advantage. It can show that a county does not have to choose between business expansion and family stability. It can show that growth, properly organized, can raise the quality of life rather than diminish it.

That is the long-range vision this series proposes: an Upstate South Carolina that welcomes growth, organizes it wisely, preserves opportunity broadly, and remains one of the few places in America where prosperity still feels attainable for ordinary people. If the region chooses that path, it will not simply keep up with growth. It will turn growth into one of its greatest strengths.

Reading the RHGM Model

The discussion in this volume leads to a simple conclusion: growth management is not a single decision, a single ordinance, or a single infrastructure standard. It is a balancing problem. Regions do not succeed merely by approving growth or restricting it. They succeed by understanding the forces that shape housing supply, affordability, infrastructure demand, and long-term community stability.

The Rational High-Growth Management model is intended to make that balancing problem visible.

At the center of the model is housing supply. This placement is deliberate. A growing region can absorb many pressures if it continues to add housing in a timely, predictable, and sufficiently broad way. But when housing supply is constricted—whether by delay, rigidity, poor planning, underbuilt infrastructure, or rising capital costs—the effects spread outward quickly. Prices rise, affordability falls, land markets distort, smaller builders withdraw, and growth begins to favor only those with the greatest financial resilience.

Five major forces act on that central question.

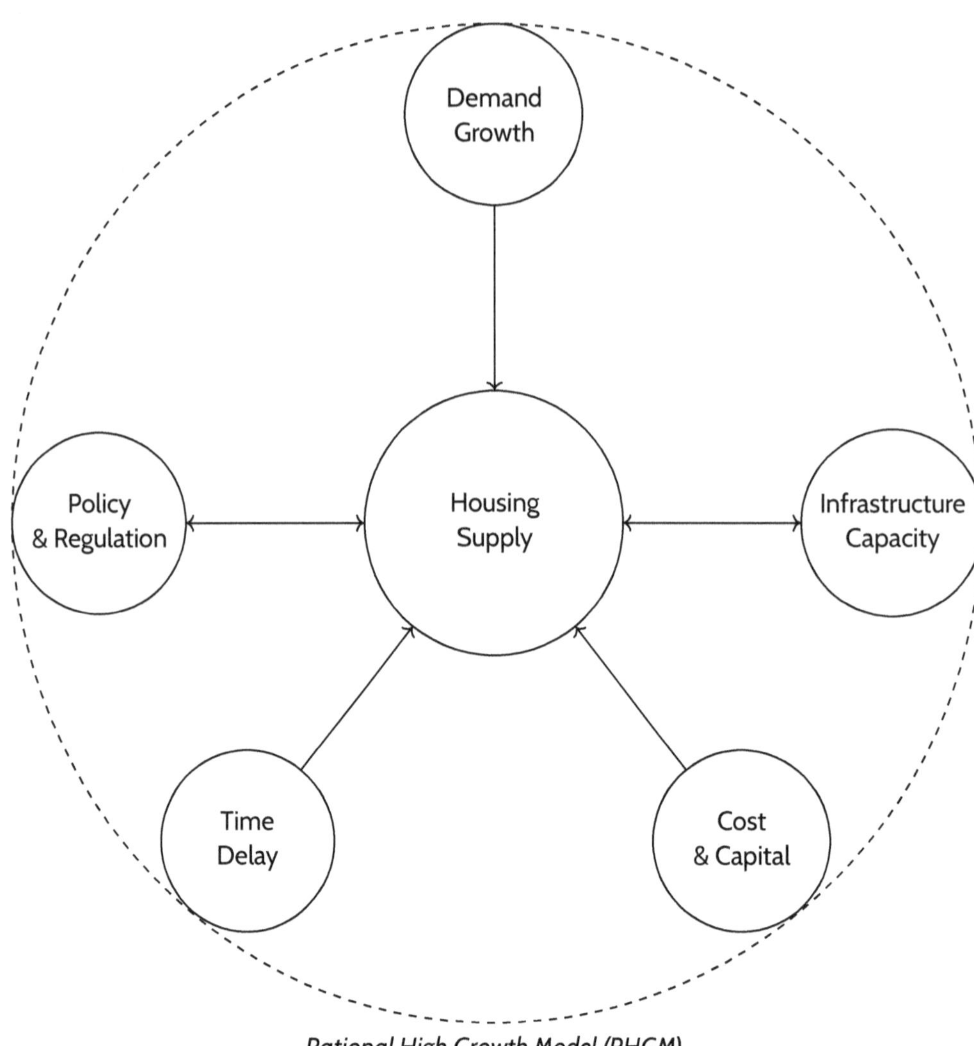

Rational High Growth Model (RHGM)

Demand growth reflects the reality that successful regions attract people, employers, and investment. Growth itself is not a problem. In many respects, it is evidence of economic vitality and regional promise. But demand that rises faster than supply produces scarcity. For that reason, growth must be anticipated rather than merely observed.

Infrastructure capacity shapes where and how growth can occur responsibly. Roads, water, sewer, drainage, schools, and public safety systems cannot be ignored. But infrastructure constraints do not solve themselves, and they should not become a disguised tool for indefinite delay. Rational growth management requires honest measurement, forward planning, and practical sequencing so that development and infrastructure can advance together.

Policy and regulation determine whether the system remains flexible or becomes brittle. Rules can provide clarity, fairness, and discipline. They can also create uncertainty, fragmentation, and artificial scarcity if they are too rigid, too slow, or too poorly calibrated. The lesson is not that policy should be absent, but that policy should be proportionate, predictable, and aligned with the broader public interest.

Time delay is one of the most underestimated forces in growth management. Delay is not neutral. Delay changes cost, changes risk, changes who can build, and changes what can be delivered. A region that wants to preserve affordability cannot treat years of uncertainty as harmless administrative friction. Time is itself a growth-management variable.

Cost and capital influence what survives the process. Financing costs, land prices, compliance costs, and infrastructure obligations all shape the housing that gets built. If those costs rise too far, the market does not respond by producing broadly attainable homes. It responds by concentrating on projects that can absorb the burden. The result is often a narrowing of housing opportunity even in regions with strong demand.

The discussion in this volume leads to a simple conclusion: growth management is not a single decision, ordinance, or infrastructure standard. It is a balancing problem. Regions do not succeed merely by approving or restricting growth. They succeed by understanding the forces that shape housing supply, affordability, infrastructure demand, and long-term stability.

The Rational High-Growth Management model makes that balancing problem visible.

At the center of the model is housing supply. This is deliberate. A growing region can absorb significant pressure if it adds housing in a timely, predictable, and sufficiently broad way. But when supply is constrained—by delay, rigidity, poor planning, limited infrastructure, or rising capital costs—the effects spread quickly. Prices rise, affordability declines, land markets distort, smaller builders withdraw, and growth begins to favor only the most financially resilient.

Applying the RHGM Model

A Community Framework for Rational Growth

Growth management is often discussed as a set of policies, regulations, or infrastructure decisions. In practice, it is something more fundamental. It is a shared effort among the people and institutions that shape how a community evolves over time.

No single group controls the outcome. Local governments make decisions, but they do not build housing alone. Developers construct projects, but they do not define infrastructure systems. Financial institutions provide capital, but they do not determine land-use policy. Residents shape expectations, but they do not operate permitting systems or design transportation networks.

When these groups operate in isolation, growth becomes fragmented and difficult to manage. When they operate together, with a shared understanding of how the system functions, growth can be guided in ways that strengthen the community.

The Rational High-Growth Management (RHGM) model is intended to support that shared understanding. It provides a way to evaluate growth decisions not as isolated actions, but as part of an interconnected system that affects housing, infrastructure, affordability, and long-term stability.

The Community as a System

Every growth decision—whether it involves a subdivision, a corridor plan, a zoning change, or an infrastructure investment—affects multiple parts of the system at once.

At the center of that system is housing supply. Around it are the forces described in the RHGM model: demand growth, infrastructure capacity, policy and regulation, time, and capital.

But those forces do not act on their own. They are shaped by the people and institutions involved in the process.

The outcome of growth is determined by how well the system works together.

Required Participants in Growth Decisions

For growth to be managed effectively, several participants must be present in the conversation. If any of these groups are absent, underrepresented, or misaligned, the system becomes unbalanced.

- **Local Government** provides the policy framework, approval process, and long-range planning structure. It defines how decisions are made and how growth is organized.

- **Infrastructure Providers** — including transportation agencies, utilities, and public service systems — ensure that roads, water, sewer, schools, and emergency services can support development.

- **Builders and Developers** translate policy and land into actual housing and commercial space. Their ability to operate efficiently determines whether supply can respond to demand.

- **Capital Providers** — banks, lenders, and investors — make projects financially possible. Their participation depends on predictability, risk, and expected return.

- **Landowners** provide the land base on which growth occurs. Their participation determines whether land is available for development and under what conditions.

- **Residents** — both current and future — represent the human purpose of growth. They shape expectations, influence public decisions, and ultimately determine whether a community remains desirable and livable.

These participants are not adversaries by default. They are interdependent. A system that recognizes that interdependence is more likely to produce balanced outcomes.

System Attributes That Enable Balanced Growth

When these participants come together, the effectiveness of the system depends on whether certain attributes are present. These attributes are observable in how a community operates.

Predictable Approval Time

Growth systems function best when timelines are understandable and consistent. When approval processes become uncertain or prolonged, risk increases, costs rise, and smaller builders may leave the market.

Sufficient Housing Supply Pathways

A healthy system allows multiple types of housing to be built across different locations and price points. When pathways narrow, supply tightens and affordability declines.

Clear Infrastructure Sequencing

Infrastructure and development must move together. When there is no clear path for aligning roads, utilities, and services with new growth, delays and inefficiencies emerge.

Accessible Capital Across Project Sizes

A balanced system supports not only large developments but also smaller projects. When financing becomes concentrated, housing production becomes less diverse and less responsive.

Policy Flexibility Within Structure

Rules should provide clarity without becoming rigid barriers. Systems that can adapt to changing conditions are more resilient than those that rely on inflexible standards.

Regional Coordination

Growth does not stop at jurisdictional boundaries. Coordination across counties and municipalities helps ensure that decisions in one area do not create unintended consequences in another.

Recognition of Time as a Cost

Time is not neutral. Delays affect financing, pricing, and participation in the market. Systems that recognize time as a real cost are more likely to maintain affordability and stability.

Recognizing Early Warning Signs

When one or more of these attributes is missing, the effects begin to appear in observable ways.

Projects may stall or become uncertain. Housing supply may slow while demand continues to rise. Prices may increase faster than incomes. Smaller builders may withdraw, leaving only large-scale development. Infrastructure may lag behind growth, creating congestion and public frustration. Development pressure may shift from one jurisdiction to another rather than being resolved.

These are not isolated problems. They are signals that the system is out of balance.

Recognizing those signals early allows communities to adjust before conditions become difficult to reverse.

Applying the Framework in Practice

The RHGM model is most useful when applied directly to real decisions.

When evaluating a proposed policy, development, or infrastructure investment, communities can ask:

- Are all key participants represented in this discussion?

- Which part of the system is under the greatest pressure?

- Which attributes are present, and which are missing?

- What outcomes are already beginning to appear?

- How will this decision affect housing supply, infrastructure alignment, and affordability over time?

These questions do not produce automatic answers. They provide a structure for better decisions.

A Shared Path Forward

Growth is not something that happens to a community. It is something a community shapes.

The Upstate of South Carolina is in a position to bring these participants together—local governments, infrastructure providers, builders, capital sources, landowners, and residents—and to approach growth as a shared responsibility rather than a series of disconnected decisions.

When that happens, growth can be guided rather than resisted, organized rather than fragmented, and aligned with the long-term interests of the region.

The purpose of the RHGM framework is not to replace local judgment. It is to support it.

It provides a common language for discussing growth, a structure for identifying imbalance, and a way for communities to work together toward outcomes that preserve opportunity, affordability, and quality of life.

Rational growth management is not simply a policy choice. It is a community choosing to act as a system.

Closing Note

The purpose of this volume is not to oppose growth, nor to endorse unmanaged expansion. It is to contribute to a shared effort: finding a practical, balanced path to success for our communities. This means advancing a rational, family-centered, and infrastructure-aware approach to high-growth management—one suited to Upstate South Carolina and to every county along or adjacent to the Interstate 85 corridor.

We are not separate places facing isolated decisions. We are a connected region experiencing the same pressures, the same opportunities, and the same responsibility to get this right. From one county to the next, we are working toward a common goal: to serve both current residents and those who will join our communities in the years ahead, while preserving the conditions that make this region a place where families can build, live, and thrive.

About the Author

Dennis C. Hayes is a native of Spartanburg, South Carolina, whose family has lived in the Upstate region for more than 280 years. Growing up in Spartanburg, becoming an eagle scout, and developing a ruby laser as his senior science project, he graduated Spartanburg High School in 1968. He left to attend Georgia Tech where he studied Physics and Computer Science. This deep-rooted connection to place has shaped both his perspective and his long-term commitment to strengthening the Upstate region's economic and technological future.

Hayes is best known for his role in creating the dial-up PC modem through his company, Hayes Microcomputer Products, which was based in Norcross, Georgia, in Technology Park—an early hub of innovation that is now part of Peachtree Corners, one of the largest cities in Gwinnett County. Through the invention of the Hayes Smartmodem and the development of the Hayes standard AT command set, his company established the technical and operational foundation for computer-to-computer communication over telephone networks. These innovations became the industry standard and played a central role in enabling the early expansion of the internet, providing millions of users with their first practical access to digital connectivity.

During the rapid growth of the Atlanta technology region in the late 1970s, 1980s and 1990s, Hayes was actively engaged not only as a business leader but also in public service. He served on the Governor's Council for Science and Technology in Georgia, contributing to discussions and initiatives that supported the development of a thriving high-technology economy. This period gave him firsthand experience with how coordinated investment, infrastructure, education, and private-sector leadership can work together to build a successful innovation ecosystem.

After decades of building and leading technology ventures, Hayes returned to Spartanburg in 2014 with a clear purpose: to help apply the lessons learned from high-growth regions like Atlanta to the Upstate of South Carolina. Recognizing the strategic importance of the corridor between Clemson and Charlotte—anchored along Interstate 85—he became deeply involved in innovation and entrepreneurial development across the region.

Hayes has emphasized the importance of "system-level thinking" in economic and entrepreneurial development. Based on his experience, he believes that beneficial growth does not happen by accident; it requires a structured, disciplined approach to planning, execution, and continuous improvement. His work focuses on helping communities, institutions, and entrepreneurs better understand how to align resources, develop talent, support early-stage ventures, and create the conditions necessary for long-term success. Through his leadership in multiple initiatives, including SPARTANSFIRST and the American Technology Venture Lab (ATVL), Hayes has worked to connect experienced mentors with emerging entrepreneurs, encourage practical commercialization of science and technology, and build a more coordinated and effective regional innovation system.

Today, Dennis C. Hayes continues to advocate for a thoughtful, structured approach to innovation-driven economic development—one that leverages the unique strengths of the Upstate region while positioning it for sustained growth in an increasingly technology-driven world. The purpose of his work is clear: to ensure that the Upstate region and Spartanburg County remain a great place to live, a wonderful place to grow a business, and the kind of community where families can thrive and prosper.

www.ingramcontent.com/pod-product-compliance
Lightning Source LLC
Chambersburg PA
CBHW042050030726
47599CB00019B/2436